This book belongs to:

....

who then passed it on to

....

who then passed it on to

....

who then passed it on to

....

KNOWLEDGE SHOULD ALWAYS BE SHARED.

Download free kids savings charts,
saving jar wrappers, Storywise play money
and parent guides from our website.

www.storywisekids.com

DAIZI
AND HER SAVING POOL

Beneath the ocean,
 as blue as the sky,
 swam a little blue dolphin
 who was a LITTLE BIT SHY.

She didn't play much
with all the others.
She was SO MUCH SMALLER
than her sisters and brothers.

But she loved TO DANCE, and she loved TO SING!

With her headphones on,
she was the HAPPIEST THING.

But when it was time for a meal or a munch, her brothers and sisters were the craziest bunch.

They would BASH,

and they would BUMP.

Food was always a fight.

Daizi mostly got nothing,

NOT EVEN A BITE.

So she had an idea,
 she thought it was COOL
to save some fish
 in a secret pool.

With a FLIP and a FLICK
and a toss and a flop,
she would kick them up
and in they would drop.

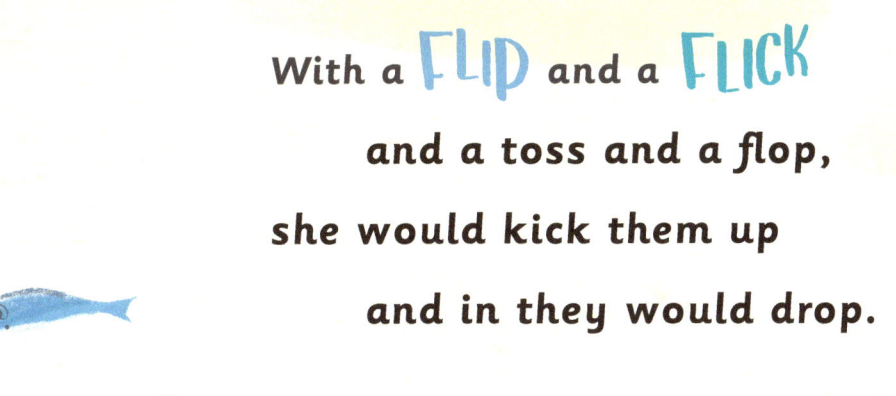

Daizi made up a song
 TO REMIND HER TO SAVE.
You could hear her sing
 as she danced on a wave.

'SAVE THE FIRST ONE FIRST, straight into the pool.

Save the first one first, it's my new saving rule.
Save the first one first, then enjoy the next four.
If you save like this, THERE WILL ALWAYS BE MORE.'

Then boats with big nets came and scooped up the school. It was so clear to Daizi they had NO SAVING RULE.

Fishermen kept every one
and let nothing go.
They didn't seem to care
TO SAVE FOR TOMORROW.

They wished for a meal,
but no fish could be seen.
There was NOTHING TO EAT,
where the fish had once been.

Daizi didn't talk much,
 but now she knew what to do.
She called out to her family,
 'I HAVE SOMETHING FOR YOU!'

Some of them scoffed, 'HOW COULD SHE HELP?' But they followed her down through the forest of kelp.

Down Daizi darted,
 between rocks and the weed,
  to her SECRET POOL
   so her family could feed.

They could not believe
she had saved all those fish.
She was HAPPY TO SHARE.
She had answered their wish.

So they fed on her fish until they were full, and there they agreed to abide by **HER RULE.**

'Whatever you catch,
ALWAYS SAVE THE FIRST ONE,

because you never can tell

when the fish might be gone.'

And so they agreed
to always add to her pool.

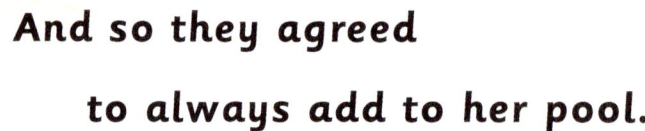

To save the first one,
it was their new savings rule.

They sang Daizi's song and saved more every day, they even had fish for their FRIENDS in the bay.

The whole family was happy.

Their tummies were full.

They had Daizi to thank for her NEW SAVING RULE.

SAVING PRINCIPLE #2

SAVE FIRST - THEN ENJOY THE REST

When you get into the great habit of saving first, you will reap great rewards. Because if you look after your savings first, they will look after you when you need them. Save today, so that you always have something for tomorrow and something you can share with others too.

WHAT CAN WE LEARN FROM DAIZI?

DISCUSSION

What great idea did Daizi have?

Daizi had a great idea to save some of the fish she caught in a secret pool so she would always have fish to eat.

DISCUSSION

What did Daizi do when the fish went away?

She took her hungry family to her secret pool and let them feast on the fish that she had saved so that they did not starve.

DISCUSSION

What did Daizi ask her family to always do from that moment on?

She asked her family to always save the first fish they caught so that they would always have some fish to eat.

FOUR SIMPLE STEPS
to start creating the right saving habits.

....

1 SET A GOAL: Find something your child really wants. Research the cost and ensure it is 'gettable' within four to six weeks with their pocket money. Remind your child that they ne to wait for the things they really want, but they will get there.

2 MAKE SAVING VISUAL: Create a saving jar. Use a glass jar so that your little saver can see their savings progress. Give them weekly pocket money (for doing simple chores) to put into the jar. Add a bit extra yourself (visible growth). Make it fun. Remind them about their goal to keep them inspired and on track.

3 DELAY GRATIFICATION: Keep them going for four to six weeks. Remind your little ones that you often need to wait for what you really want. It's about creating the right conversation and instilling the right behaviours.

4 CELEBRATE AND REPEAT: When they have reached their goal, celebrate it. Make sure they get what they were saving for and if possible, make them pay the money over to the cashier themselves. And then repeat. As they grow older you can make the goals bigger and the saving time longer.

**Visit www.storywisekids.com
to download a kids savings planner and more.**

DOWNLOAD FREE SAVING TOOLS
at www.storywisekids.com

Find all the help and tools you need on our website under the resources tab.

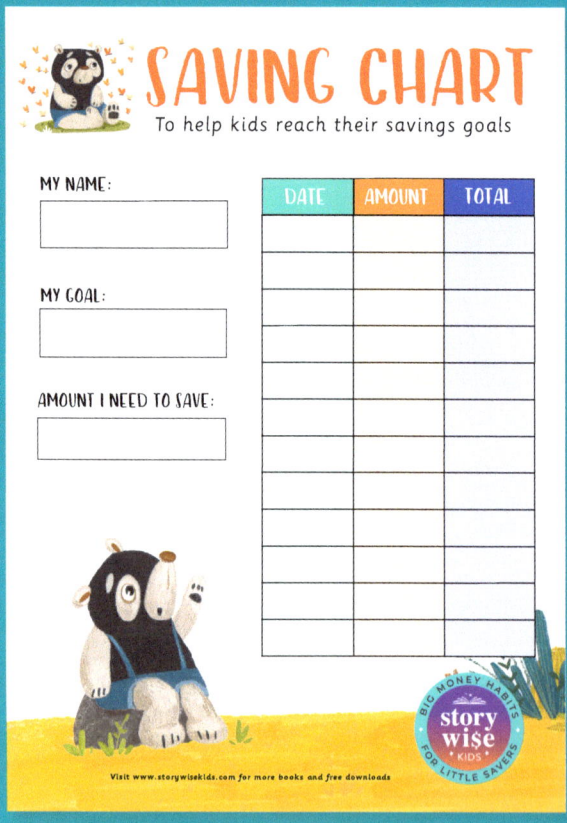

10 things parents can do to build money-wise kids

The 10 points below are a great guide for creating money-wise kids. For a more comprehensive guide visit the website.

1. Start their financial education as soon as possible
2. Let them know that money comes from work
3. Young kids learn more through observation than education - set the right example with money
4. Include them in basic money discussions
5. Share your saving journey with them
6. Embed the right principles like delayed gratification, planning ahead and self discipline
7. Avoid debt – never give them a loan. Ever!
8. When it's gone - it is gone. Money supply is not endless
9. Introduce the importance of giving
10. Parents need to be on the same page

For Bella and her friends

Written by Doug Lockhart
Illustrations by Marina Zorina

Edited by Natalie Bell

First published in 2021 by STORYWISE KIDS
Sunset Beach, Milnerton, 7441, Cape Town, South Africa

Concept, text and illustrations copyright © Doug Lockhart 2021.

All rights reserved. No part of this publication may be reproduced, stored in a retrieval system, or transmitted, in any form or by any means (electronic, mechanical, photocopying, recording or otherwise), without the prior permission of the publisher.

ISBN 978-1-77630-133-1 (paperback)
ISBN 978-1-77630-132-4 (ebook)
ISBN 978-1-77630-134-8 (hardcover)

A copy of this book can be found at the
National Library of South Africa Pretoria Campus.

www·storywisekids·com

www.ingramcontent.com/pod-product-compliance
Lightning Source LLC
LaVergne TN
LVHW072104070426
835508LV00003B/266